50 Great Classical Guitar Solos

Arranged by Howard Wallach

ISBN: 978-1-57560-950-8

Visit our website at www.cherrylane.com

Table of Contents

Signs, Symbols, and Terms 4
    Found in this Book

Music of the Renaissance

Pavan V .... Milán 8
Pavan VI .... Milán 10
Polish Dance I .... Anonymous 12
Polish Dance II .... Anonymous 14
Villanella .... Dlugoraj 16
Finale .... Dlugoraj 18
Pavan .... Byrd 20
Mr. Dowland's Midnight .... Dowland 22
My Lord Willoughby's .... Dowland 23
    Welcome Home

Music of the Baroque Era

La Chaconna .... Vallet 24
Bourrée .... Vallet 27
Allemanda .... Calvi 29
Romanesca .... Calvi 31
Volta .... Galilei 33
Courante .... Sweelinck 36
Menuet .... de Visée 38
Bourrée .... de Visée 39
Passepied I .... Le Cocq 40
Passepied II .... Le Cocq 42
Menuet .... Handel 44
Oh Sacred Head Now Wounded .... Bach 46
Sarabande .... Bach 47
Bourrée .... Bach 49

Music of the Classic Era

Study in G Major	Aguado	51
Waltz	Aguado	53
Andantino	Carulli	55
Waltz	Carulli	57
Andante	Carulli	59
Study in A Major	Carcassi	62
Study in E Minor	Carcassi	64
Caprice	Carcassi	67
Allegretto	Giuliani	70
Andantino	Giuliani	72
Study in A Minor	Giuliani	74
Andante	Sor	76
Study in A Major	Sor	77
Study in D Major	Sor	79
Minuet	Sor	81

Music of the Romantic Era

Bagatelle	Schumann	85
Ländler I	Mertz	87
Ländler II	Mertz	89
Study in C Major	Coste	92
Study in A Minor	Coste	97
Prelude	Coste	100
Russian Song	Tchaikovsky	102
Prelude in D Major	Tárrega	104
Prelude (Endecha)	Tárrega	105
Prelude in D Minor	Tárrega	106
Prelude in E Major	Tárrega	109
Mazurka	Tárrega	111

Signs, Symbols, and Terms
Found in this Book

Right Hand Indications

p = Thumb
i = Index finger
m = Middle finger
a = Ring finger

= The notes of a given chord are to be arpeggiated (from bass to treble) with right hand fingers or thumb.

Left Hand Indications

⌢ or ⌣ = Hammer-on (H) if to a higher note, or pull-off (P) if to a lower note.

B = Bar fret indicated by Roman numeral
$\frac{1}{2}$B = Half bar
= Hinge bar
= Glissando (gliss.)

Scordaturas (Altered Tunings)

⑥ = D : Tune the 6th string down to D.

③ = F♯ : Tune the 3th string down to F♯.

Accidentals

♯ = Sharp: raises the note one fret.

✕ = Double sharp: raises the note two frets.

♭ = Flat: lowers the note one fret.

♭♭ = Double flat: lowers the note two frets.

♮ = Natural: cancels the sharp or flat.

Time Signatures $\frac{2}{4}$ $\frac{3}{4}$ $\frac{4}{4}$ $\frac{6}{8}$ C ¢

The top number indicates the number of beats per measure. The bottom number indicates which note value equals one beat. "4" on the bottom indicates that the quarter note equals one beat. "8" on the bottom indicates that the eighth note equals one beat. C stands for common time, which is the same as $\frac{4}{4}$ time. ¢ stands for cut time, which is the same as $\frac{2}{2}$ time.

Tempo Indications

Adagio = Slowly.
Allegretto = Lively; moderately quick.
Allegro = Fast; rapidly.
Andante = Moderately; at a walking pace.
Andantino = A little slower than Andante.
Larghetto = A little faster than Largo.
Largo = Quite slowly; slower than Adagio.
Lento = Slowly; between Andante and Largo.
Moderato = Moderately; at a moderate pace.

Performance Indications

⌐1.¬ ⌐2.¬	= First and second endings. Play ⌐1.¬ the first time through and play ⌐2.¬ for the repeat, omitting ⌐1.¬.
𝄆 𝄇	= Repeat signs. Play the music within these signs twice.
D.C. al Fine	= *Da Capo al Fine*. Go back to the beginning and play till the word *Fine* (end) appears.
⌒ or ⌣	= Tie signs. Joins two or more notes of the same pitch creating one longer note value.
⌢ or ⌣	= Fermata. Hold sign. Indicates that the note or chord above or below the sign should be held for longer than its written value; at the performer's discretion.

Tablature Explanation

Tablature notation graphically represents the strings and frets of the guitar fingerboard. The six lines represent the six strings of the guitar, and the numbers represent which fret to press on each string.

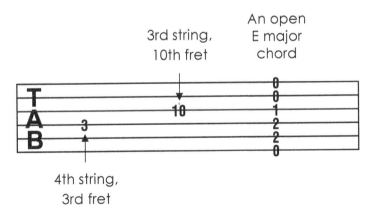

3rd string, 10th fret

An open E major chord

4th string, 3rd fret

Ornaments

There are two kinds of left hand ornaments
necessary to play the music in this book.
The first kind is the trill (*tr* or ﻬ) which is written:

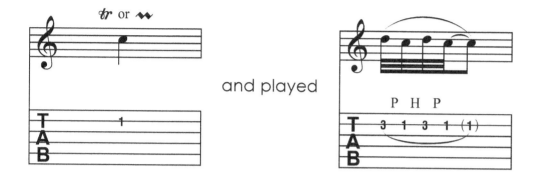

and played

The second kind is the mordent (ﻬ) which is written:

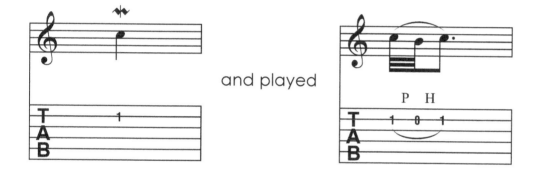

and played

Types of Dances and Pieces

Pavan = A dance of Italian origin popular in the 16th and 17th centuries. It was in simple duple time and of stately character.

Villanella = Street song popular in the 16th Century, also a type of part-song less complex than the madrigal.

Finale = The last movement of a work in several movements.

Chaconna = Originally a dance of 3-in-a-measure rhythms, with the music built on (over) a ground bass. Sometimes there is no actual ground bass, but the music falls into a number of short sections similar to those written over a ground bass.

Bourée = A lively dance in quadruple time beginning with an up beat.

Allemanda = A dance usually in $\frac{4}{4}$, but sometimes in duple meter. Often found as the first dance of a suite. It is serious in character and of moderate speed.

Romanesca = 1) A kind of galliard from Romagna.

2) A certain melody popular in the 17th Century as a ground bass.

Volta = A quick dance in triple meter; also known as "Lavolta" or "LaVolta," similar to the galliard.

Courante = A French dance popular in the 17th and 18th centuries and commonly found in the baroque suite. There are two types:
1) The Italian variety: rapid tempo in simple triple time.
2) The French variety: similar to the Italian, but with a different character and in quadruple meter.

Menuet = A stately court dance of the 17th and 18th centuries in triple time. It was an optional movement of the suite and is found later in the classical symphonies of Haydn and Mozart.

Passepied = A lively dance in $\frac{3}{8}$ or $\frac{6}{8}$ time, which originated amongst French sailors, and later became popular at court.

Sarabande = A slow and stately dance form in triple time. It was a standard movement of the baroque suite. There had existed an earlier, lively version.

Waltz = A dance in $\frac{3}{4}$ time which came into prominence in the last quarter of the 18th Century. It rose to tremendous popularity in the 19th Century, especially in Vienna.

Caprice = A light, quick composition with an improvisational feel, often including striking or original effects.

Bagatelle = A short unpretentious instrumental composition; a trifle.

Ländler = A type of slow waltz originating in northern Austria.

Prelude = A piece of music which precedes something else. In the 19th and 20th centuries, a self-contained short instrumental piece which sets a mood.

Mazurka = A traditional Polish country dance in triple time with an accentuation of the second beat of each measure and an ending of the phrases on that beat.

Pavan V

Luys Milán
(16th Century)

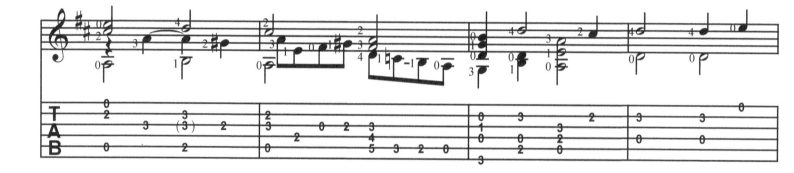

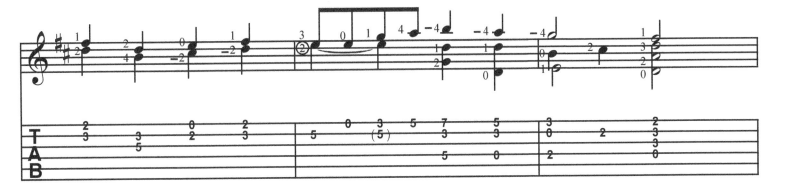

Pavan VI

Luys Milán
(16th Century)

Polish Dance I

Anonymous
(16th Century)

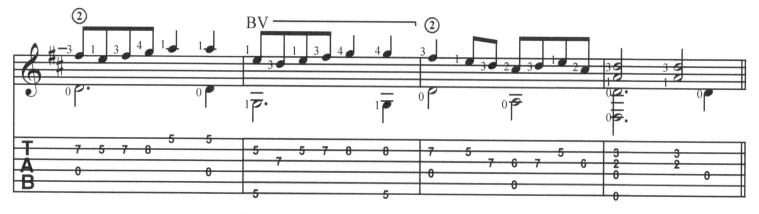

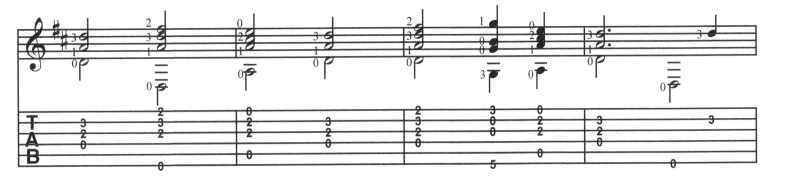

Polish Dance II

Anonymous
(16th Century)

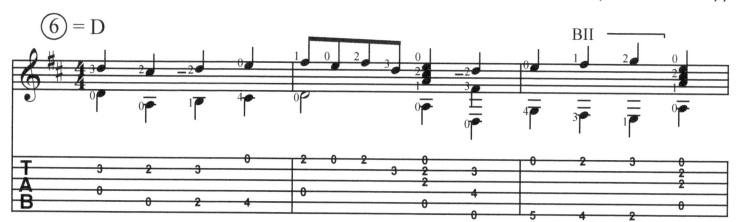

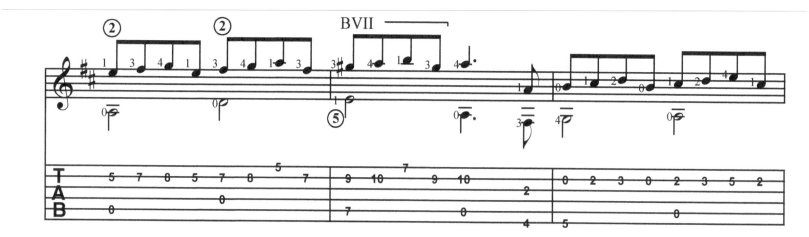

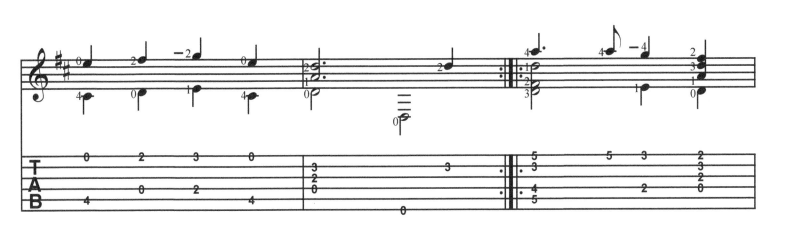

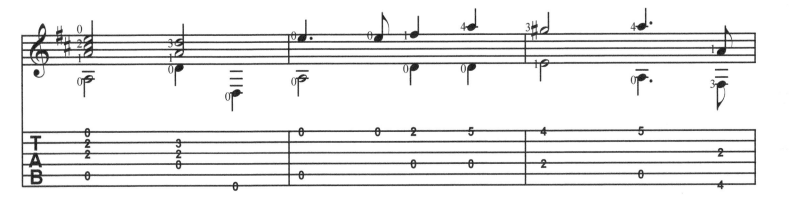

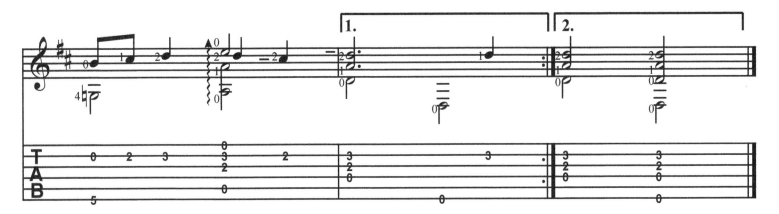

Villanella

Wojciech Dlugoraj
(1550 - ca. 1619)

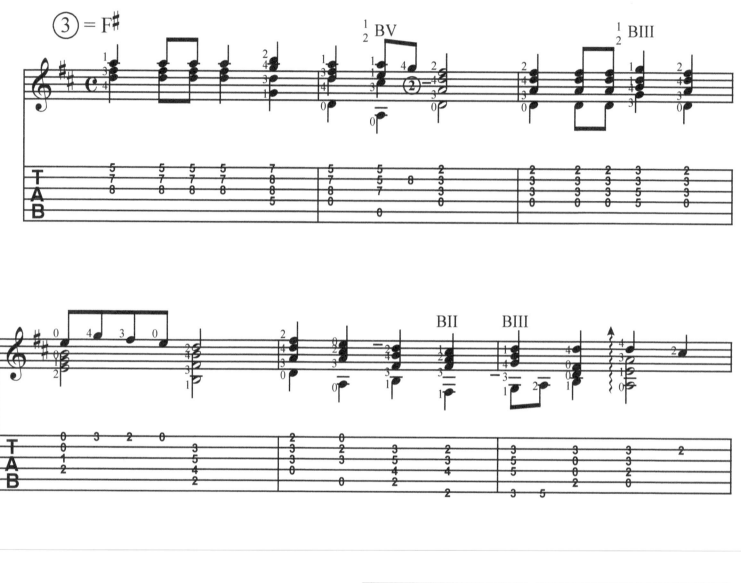

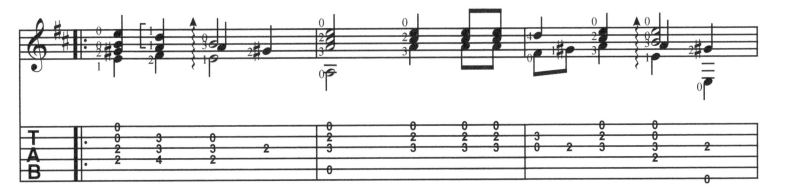

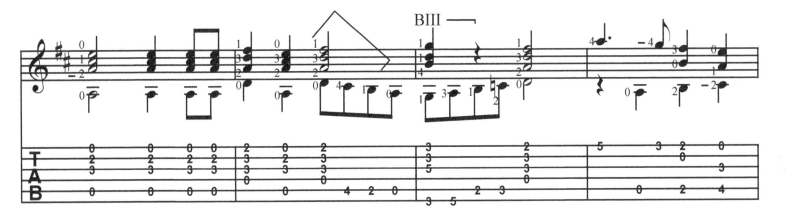

Finale

Wojciech Dlugoraj
(1550 - ca. 1619)

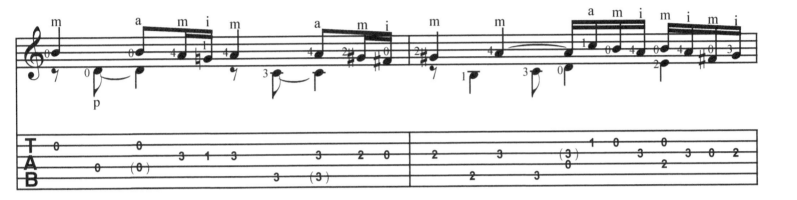

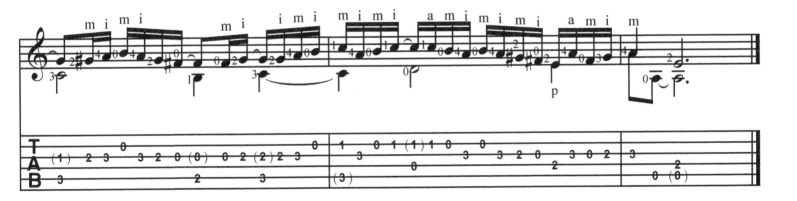

Pavan

William Byrd
(1543-1623)

Mr. Dowland's Midnight

John Dowland
(1563-1626)

My Lord Willoughby's Welcome Home

John Dowland
(1563-1626)

La Chaconna

Nicolas Vallet
(ca. 1553-1626)

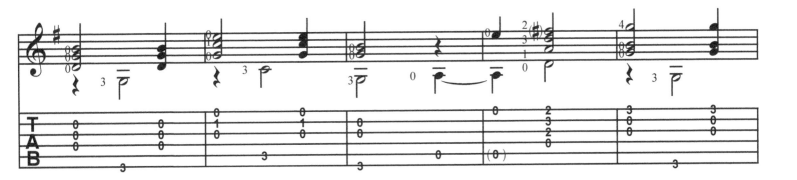

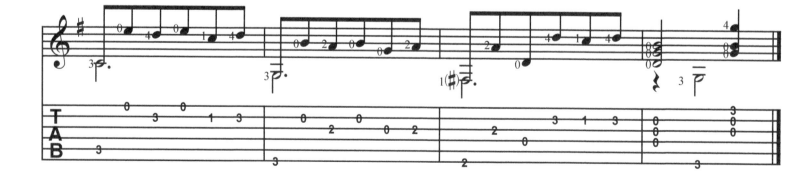

Bourrée

Nicolas Vallet
(ca. 1553-1626)

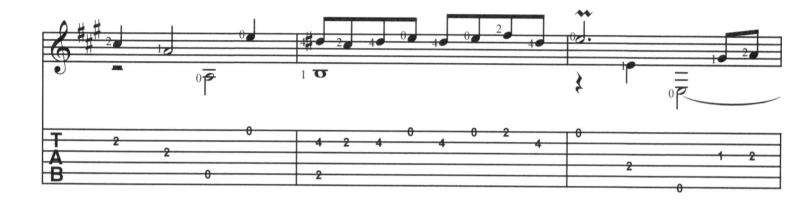

Allemanda

Carlo Calvi
(17th Century)

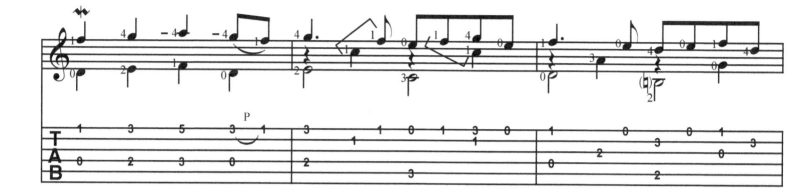

Romanesca

Carlo Calvi
(17th Century)

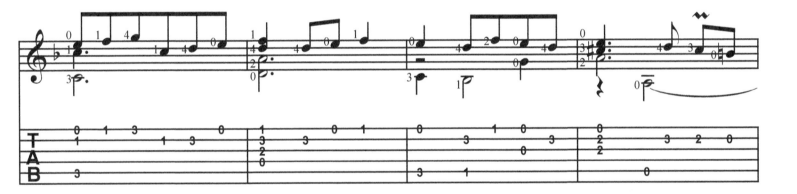

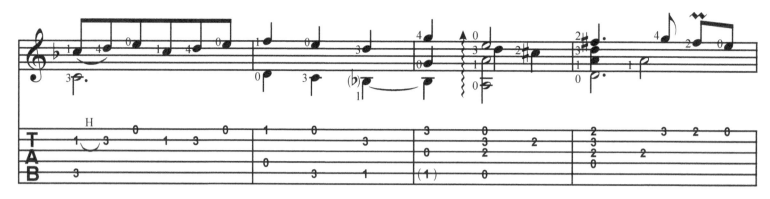

Volta

Michelangelo Galilei
(1575-1631)

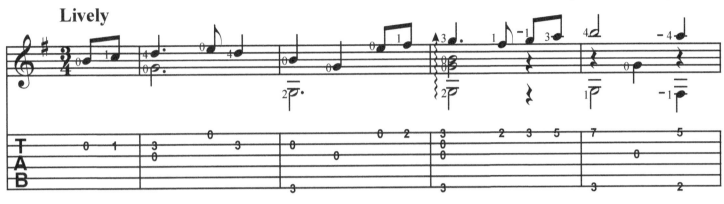

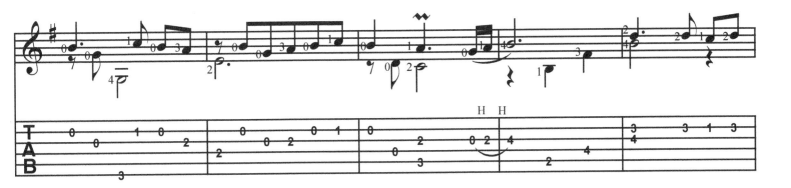

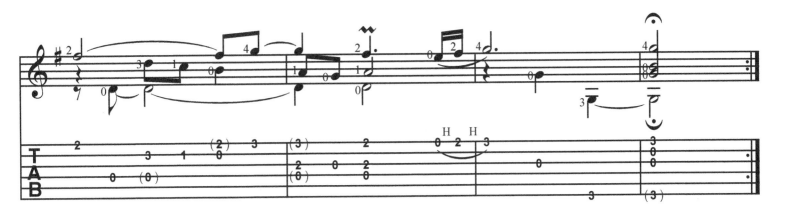

Courante

J. P. Sweelinck
(1562-1621)

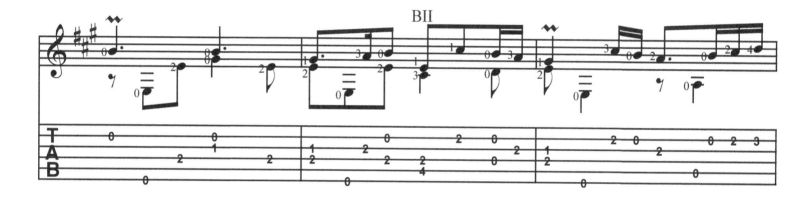

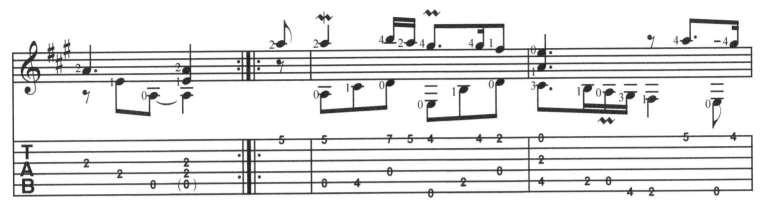

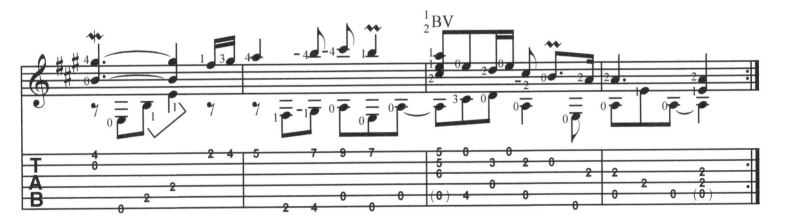

Menuet

Robert de Visée
(1650-1725)

Bourrée

Robert de Visée
(1650-1725)

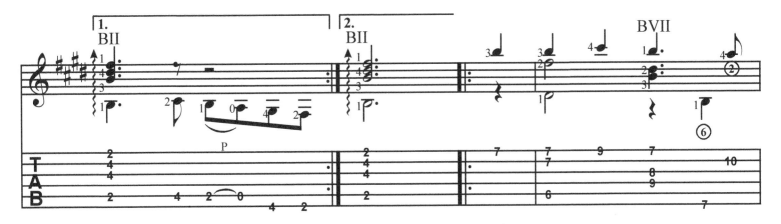

Passepied I

François Le Cocq
(1679-1730)

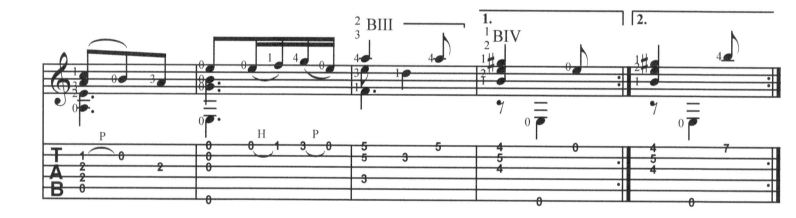

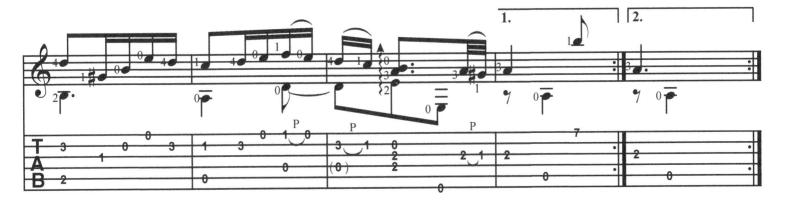

Passepied II

François Le Cocq
(1679-1730)

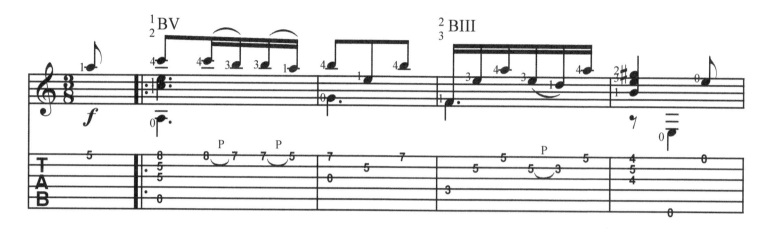

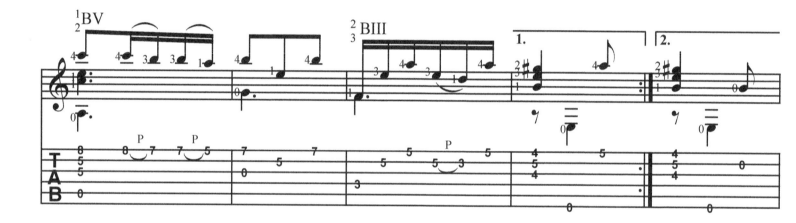

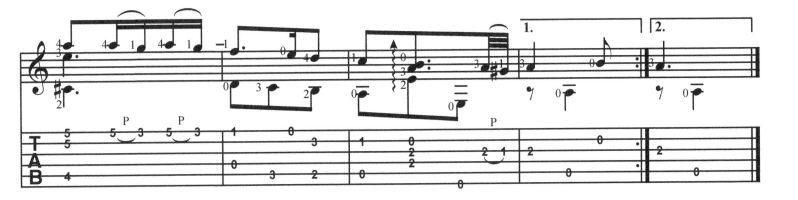

Menuet

George Friedrich Handel
(1685-1759)

Oh Sacred Head Now Wounded
from *St. Matthew Passion*

J. S. Bach
(1685-1750)

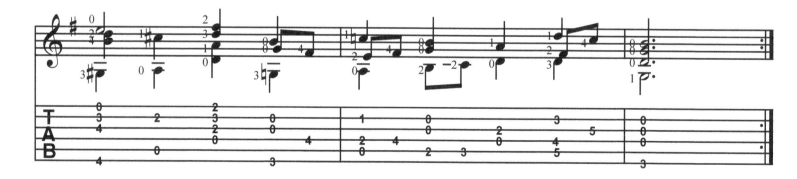

Sarabande

J. S. Bach
(1685-1750)

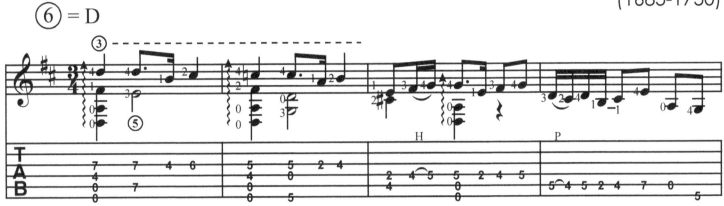

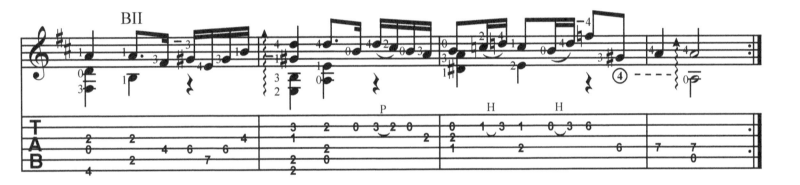

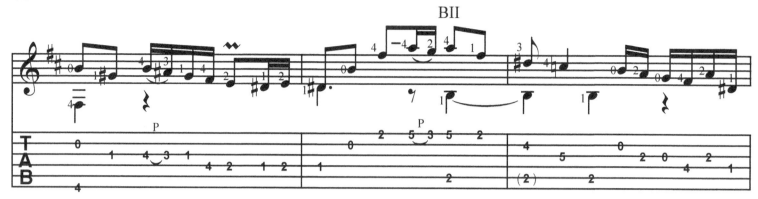

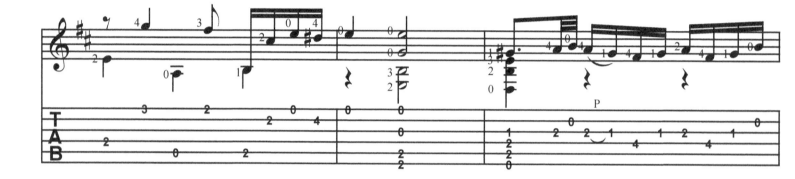

Bourrée
from *Cello Suite No. 3*

J. S. Bach
(1685-1750)

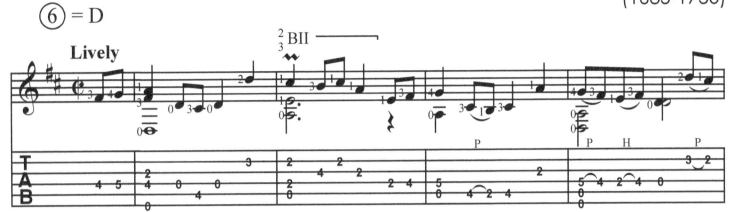

Study in G Major

Dionisio Aguado
(1784-1849)

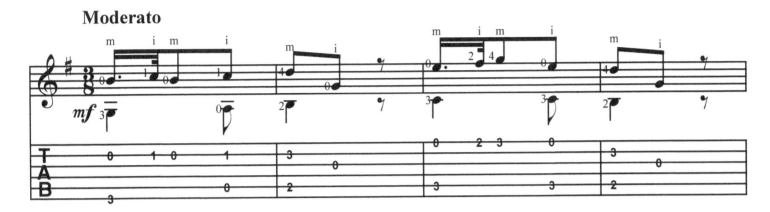

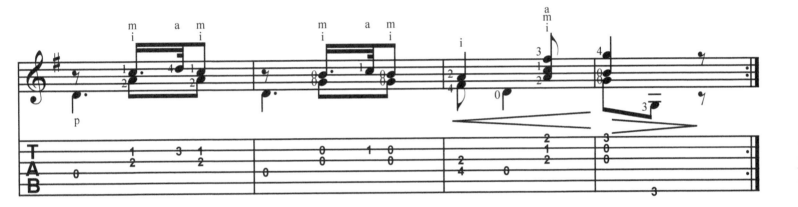

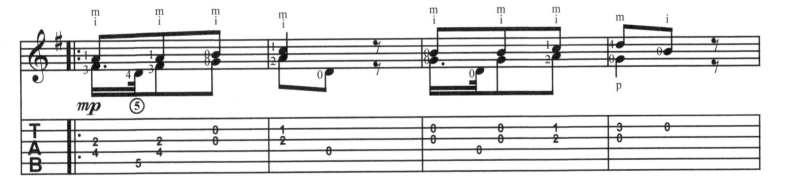

52

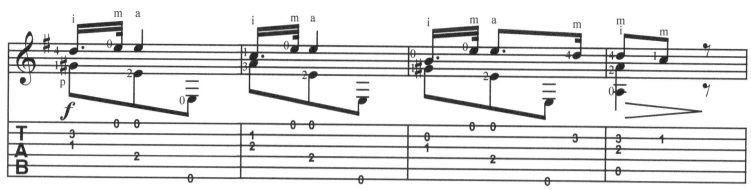

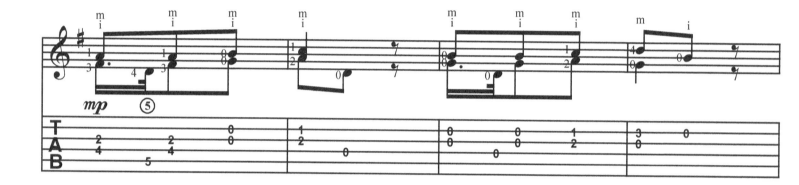

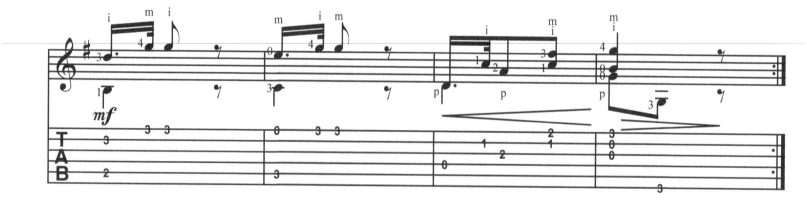

Waltz

Dionisio Aguado
(1784-1849)

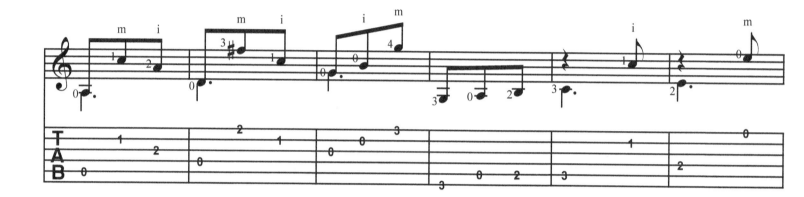

Andantino

Ferdinando Carulli
(1770-1841)

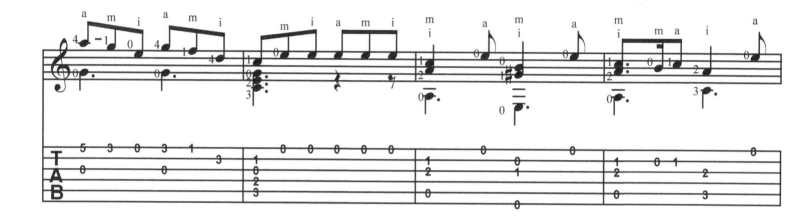

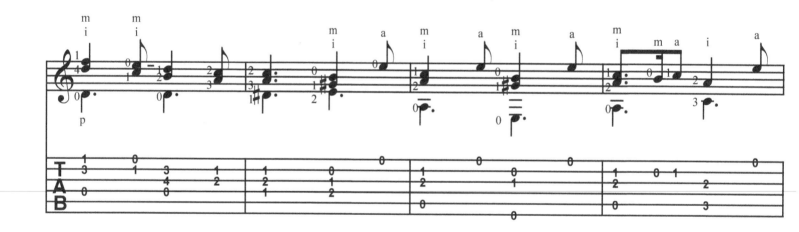

Waltz

Ferdinando Carulli
(1770-1841)

D. C. al Fine

Andante

Ferdinando Carulli
(1770-1841)

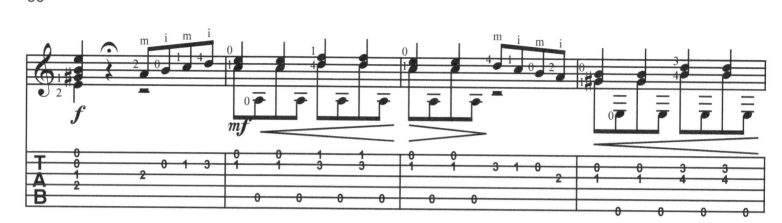

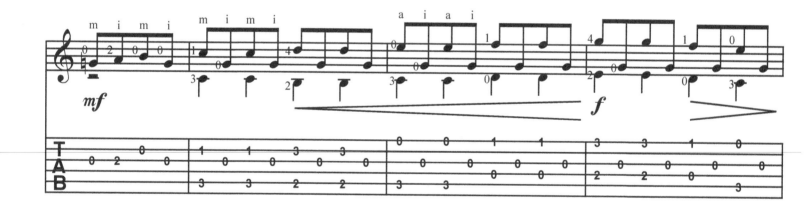

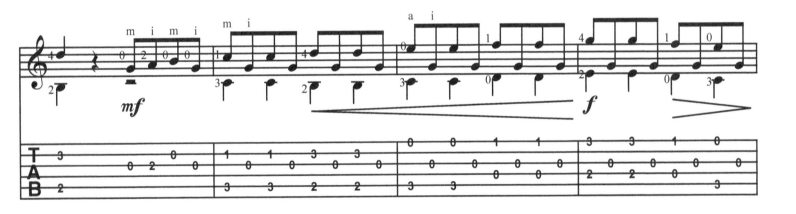

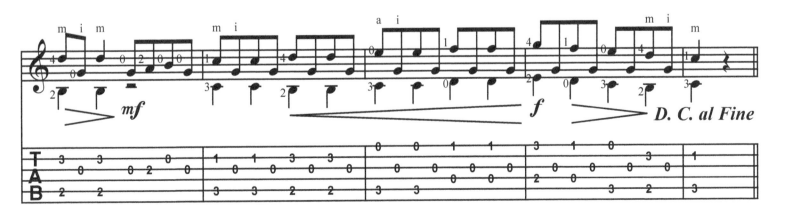

Study in A Major

Matteo Carcassi
(1792-1853)

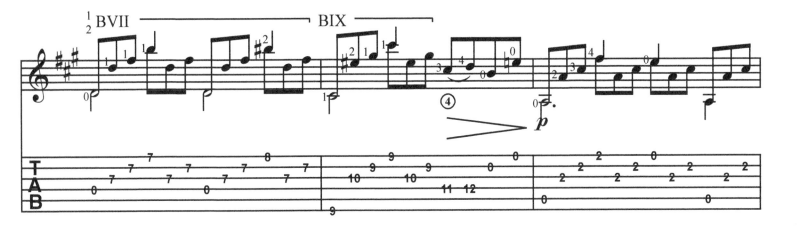

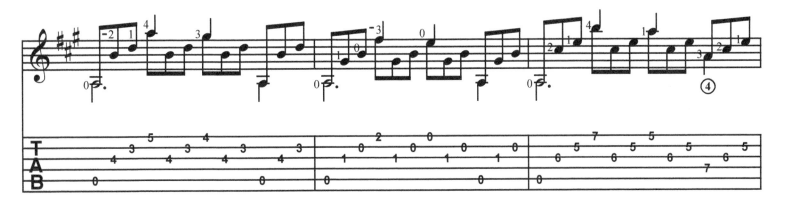

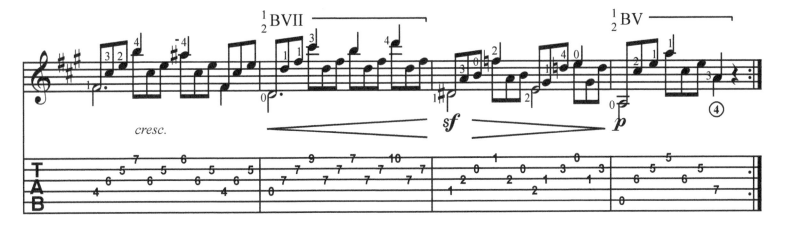

Study in E Minor

Matteo Carcassi
(1792-1853)

Allegro moderato

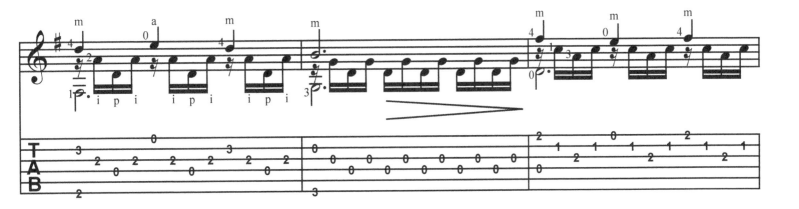

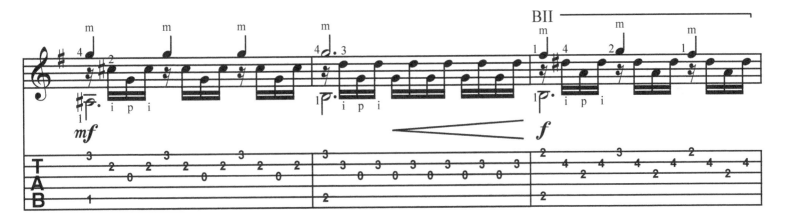

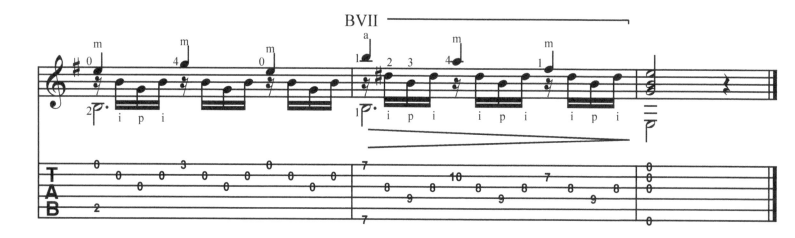

Caprice

Matteo Carcassi
(1792-1853)

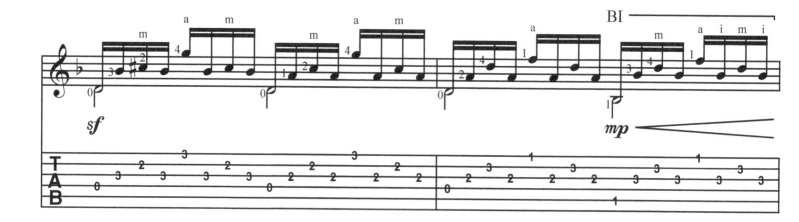

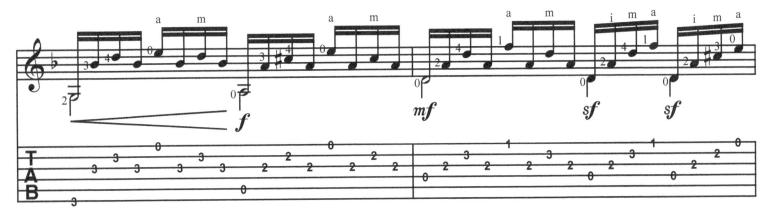

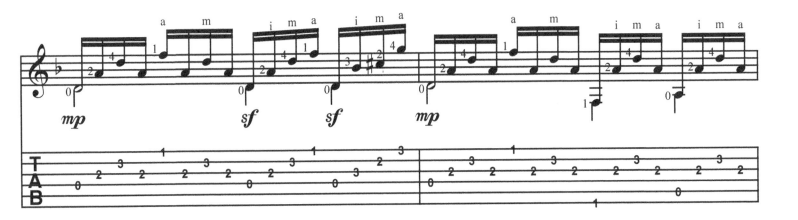

Allegretto

Mauro Giuliani
(1781–1829)

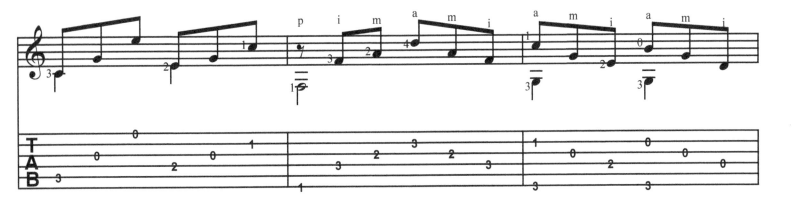

Andantino

Mauro Giuliani
(1781-1829)

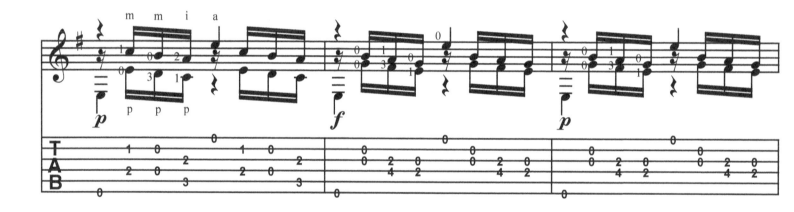

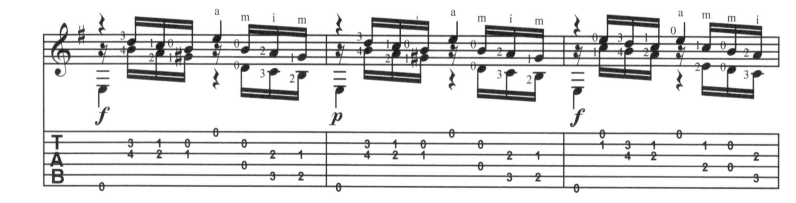

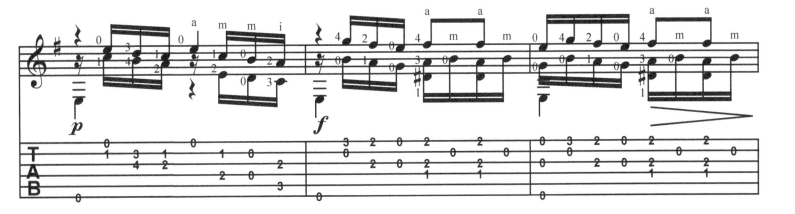

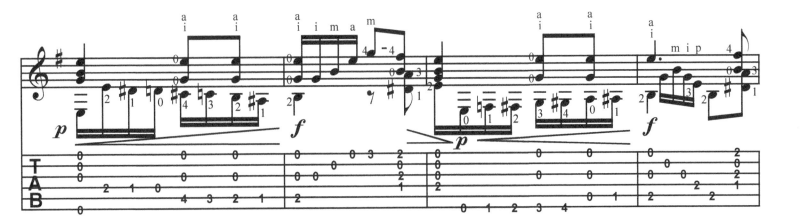

Study in A Minor

Mauro Giuliani
(1780-1829)

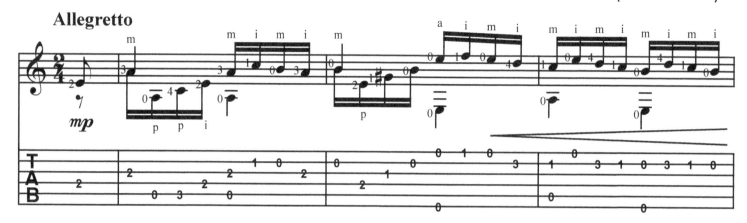

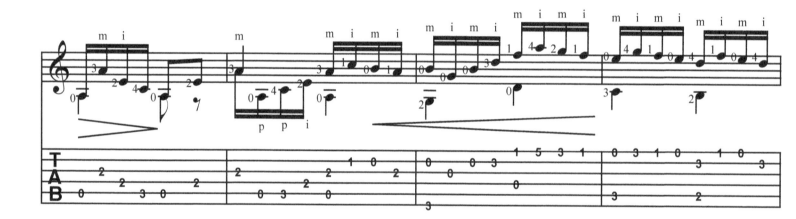

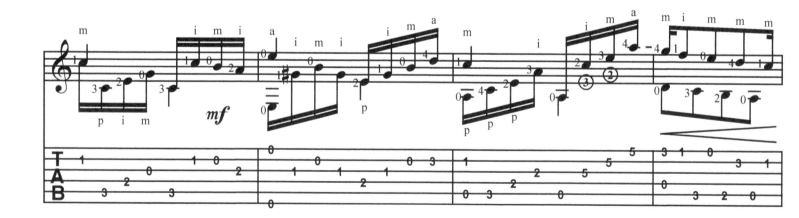

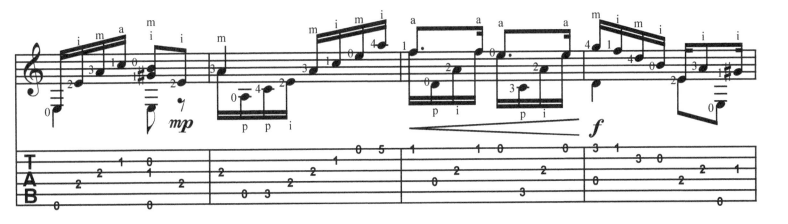

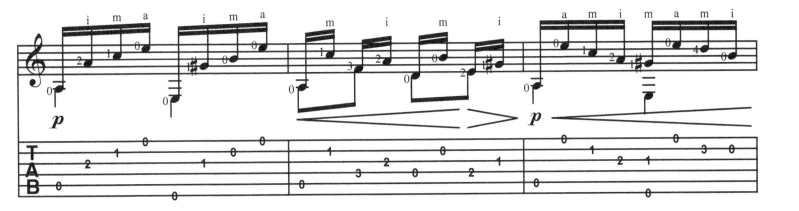

Andante

Fernando Sor
(1778-1839)

Study in A Major

Fernando Sor
(1778-1839)

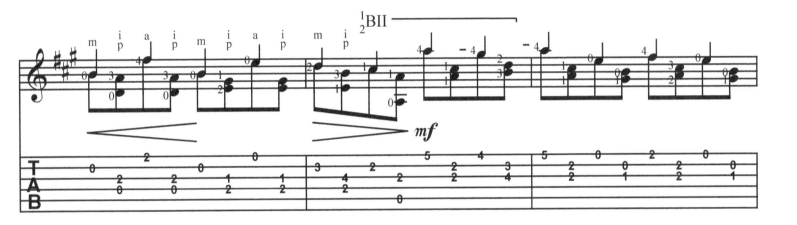

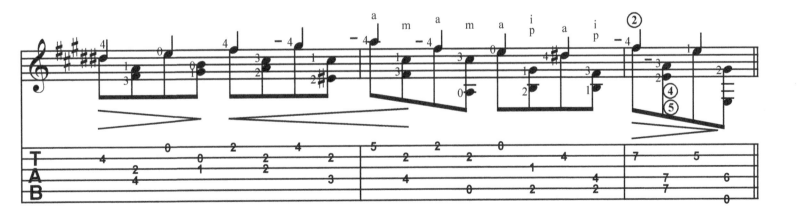

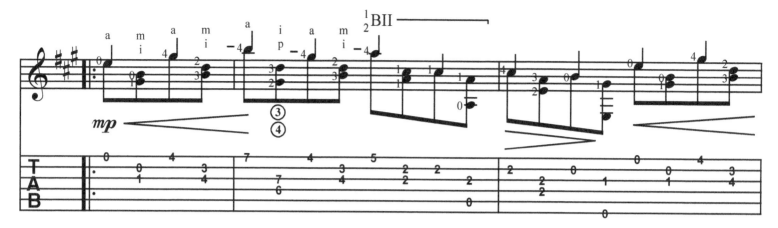

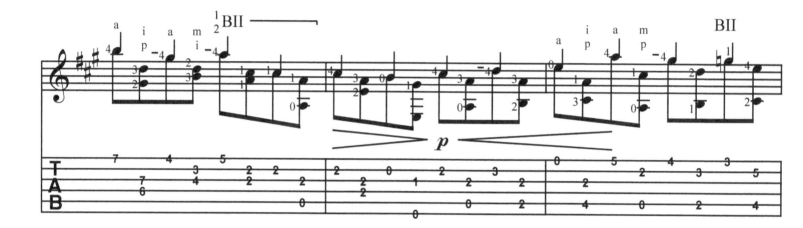

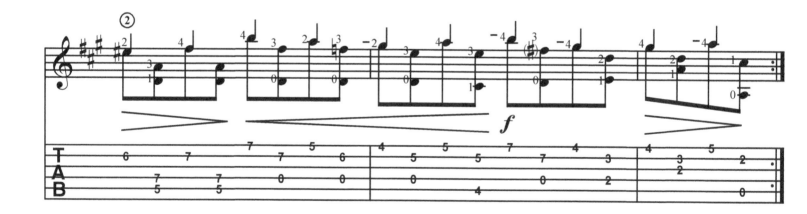

Study in D Major

Fernando Sor
(1778-1839)

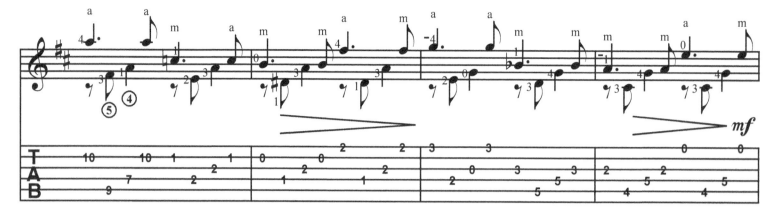

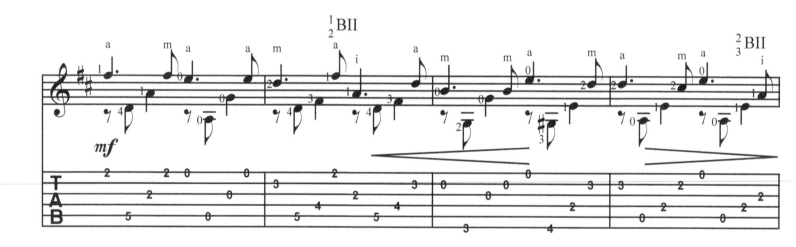

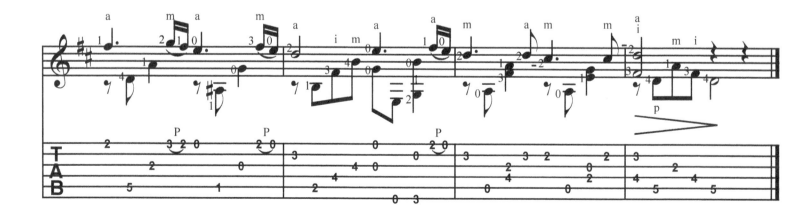

Minuet

Fernando Sor
(1778-1839)

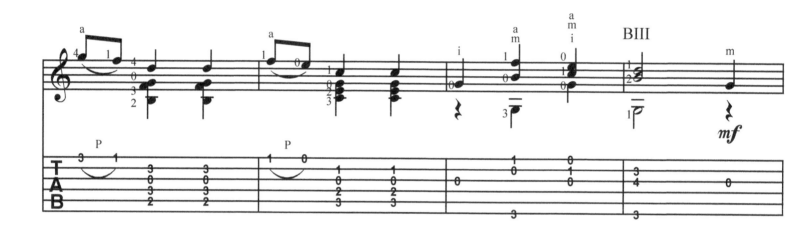

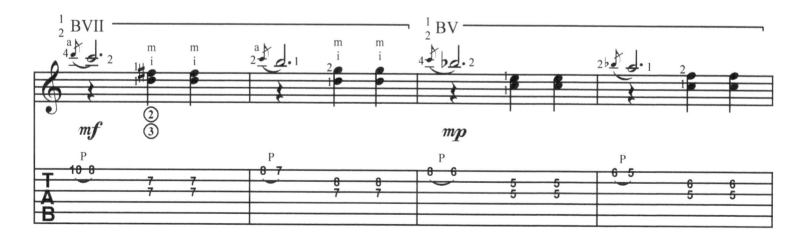

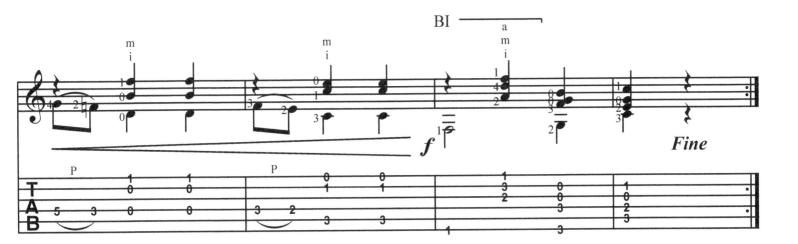

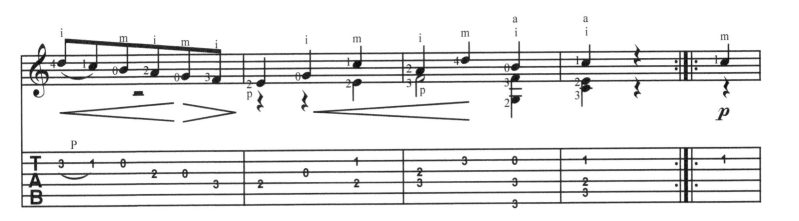

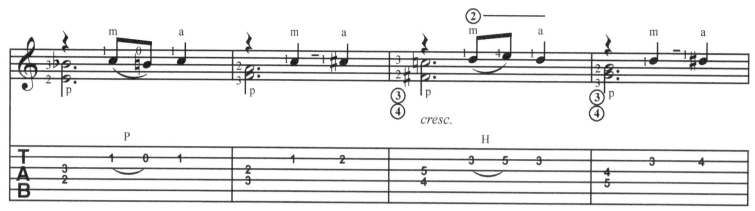

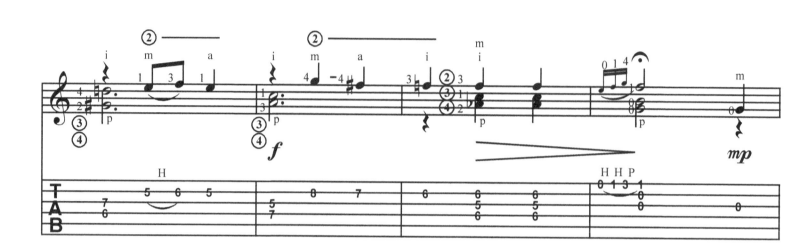

Bagatelle

Robert Schumann
(1810-1856)

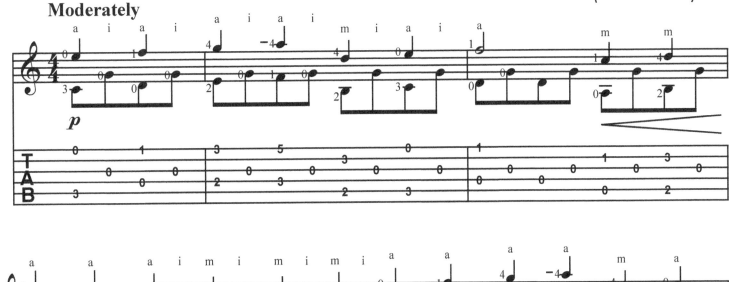

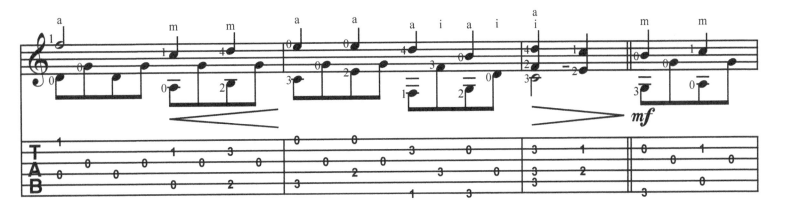

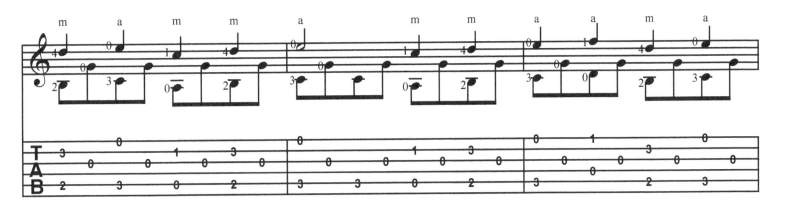

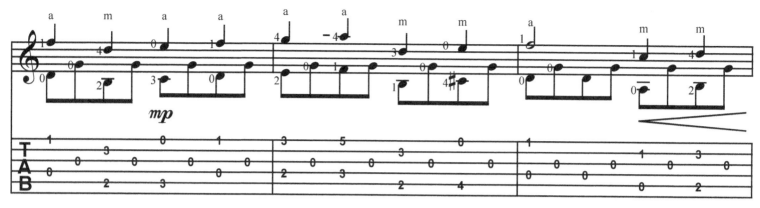

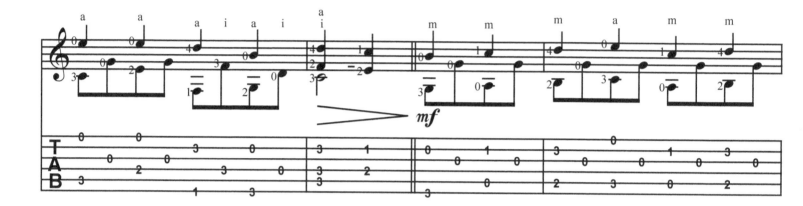

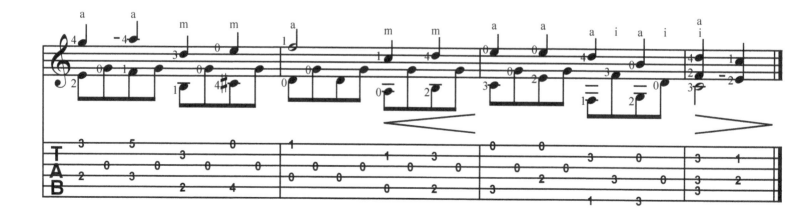

Ländler I

Johann Kaspar Mertz
(1806-1856)

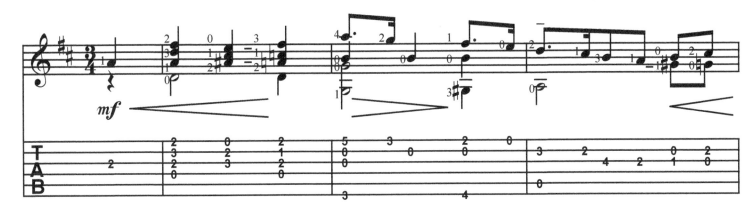

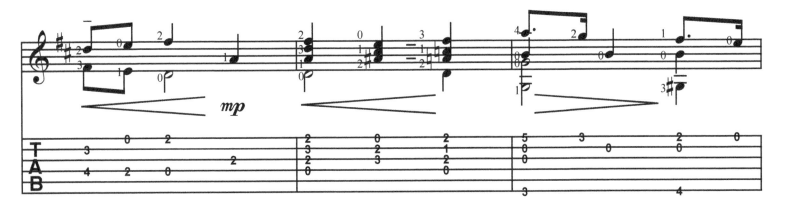

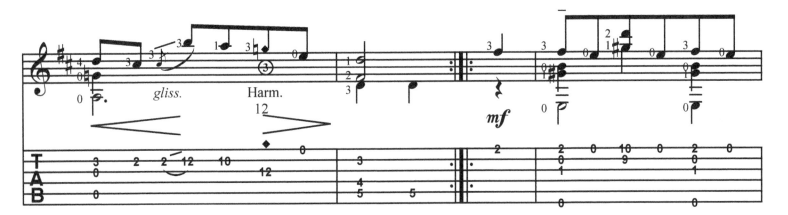

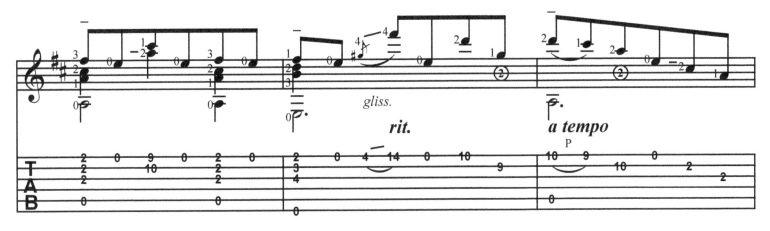

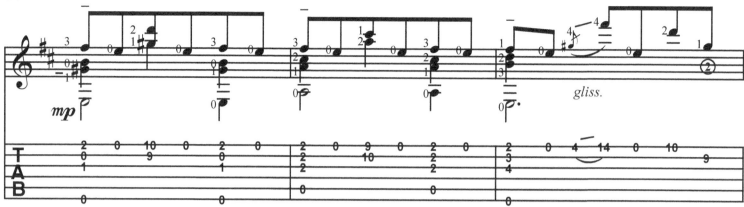

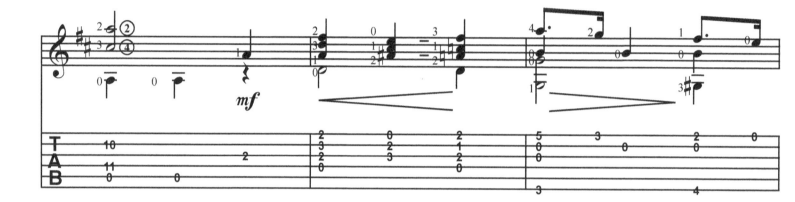

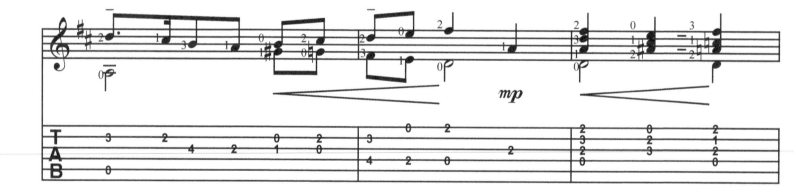

Ländler II

Johann Kaspar Mertz
(1806-1856)

90

Study in C Major

Napoleon Coste
(1806-1883)

Allegretto

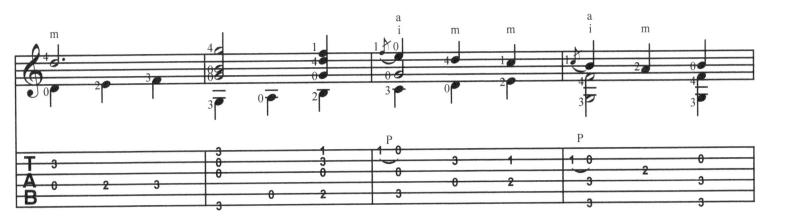

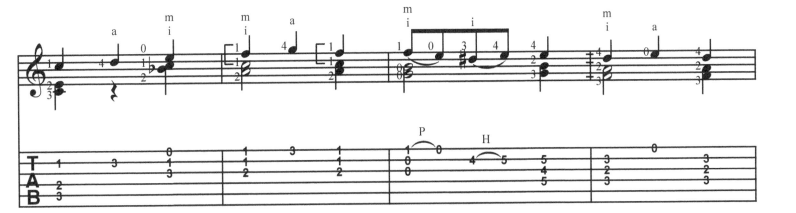

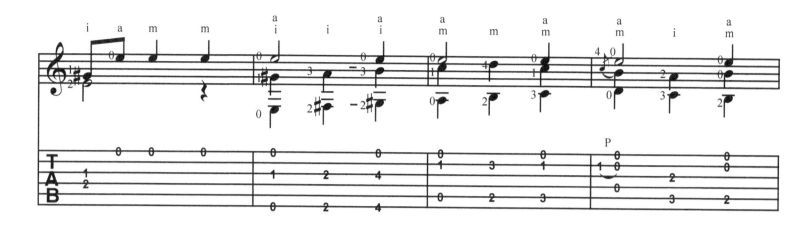

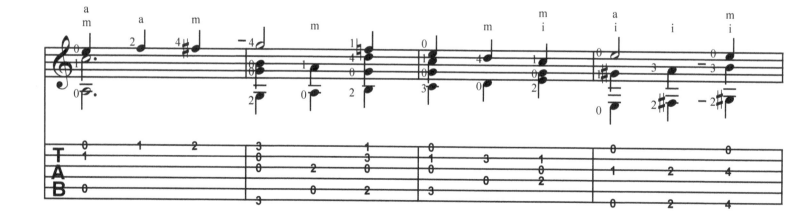

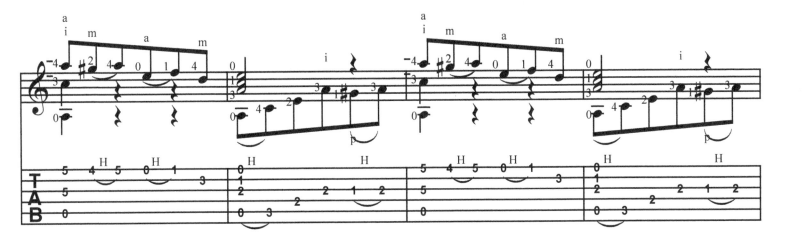

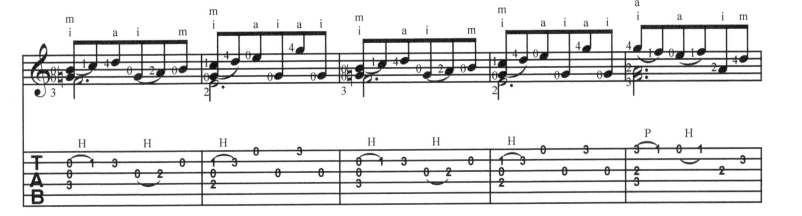

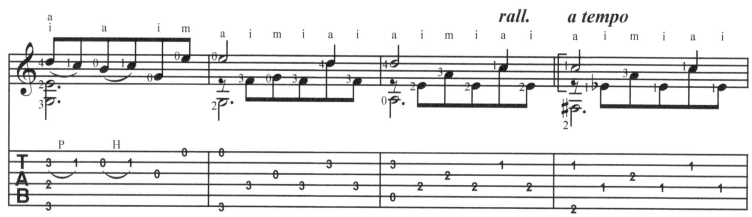

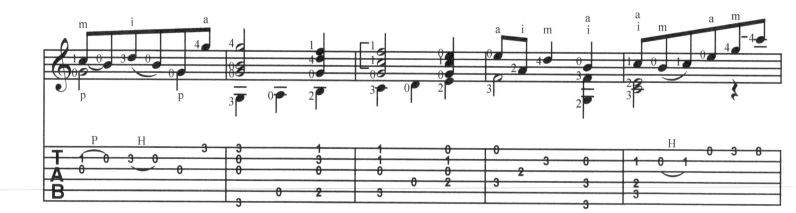

Study in A Minor

Napoleon Coste
(1806-1883)

Allegretto

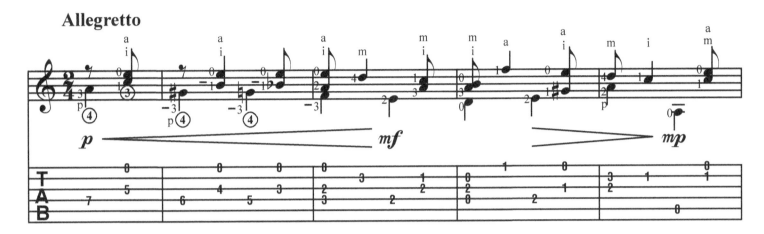

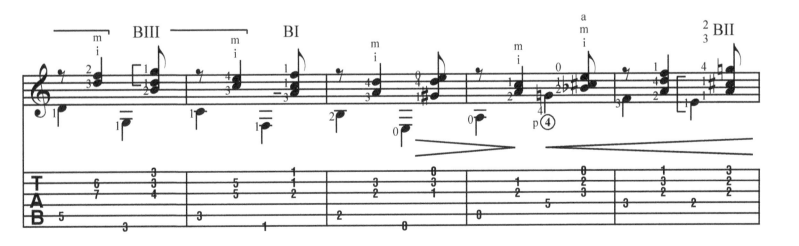

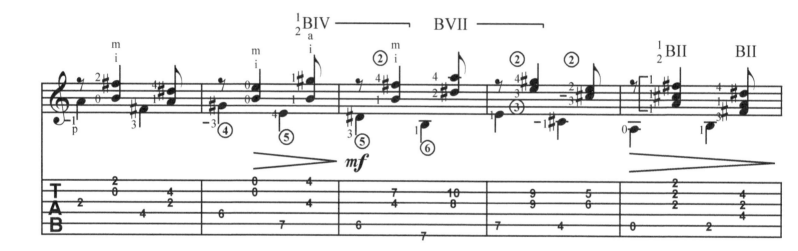

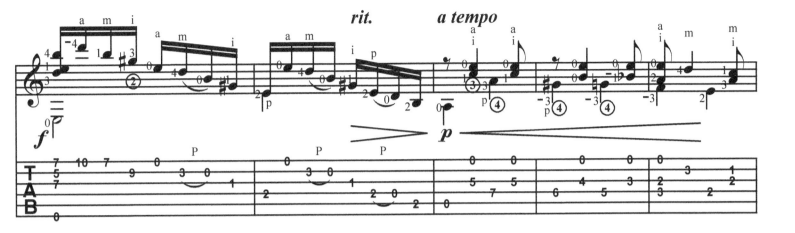

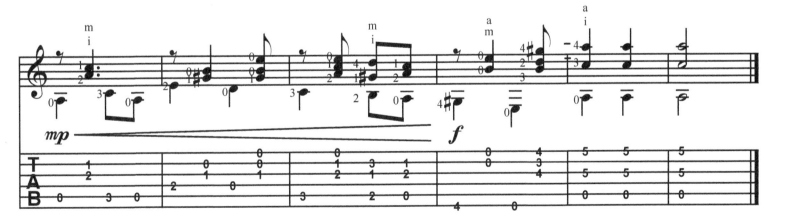

Prelude

Napoleon Coste
(1806-1883)

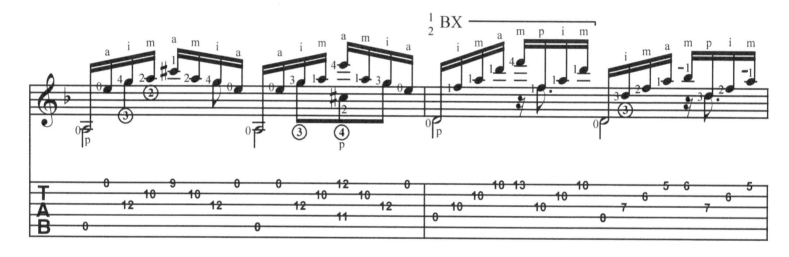

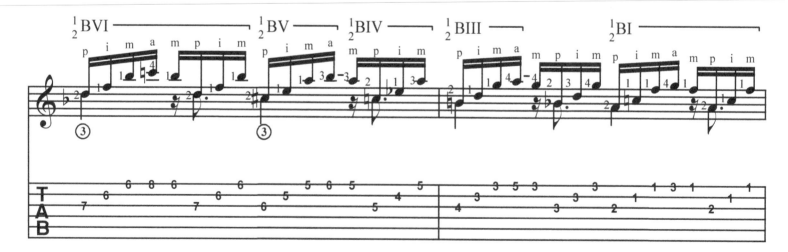

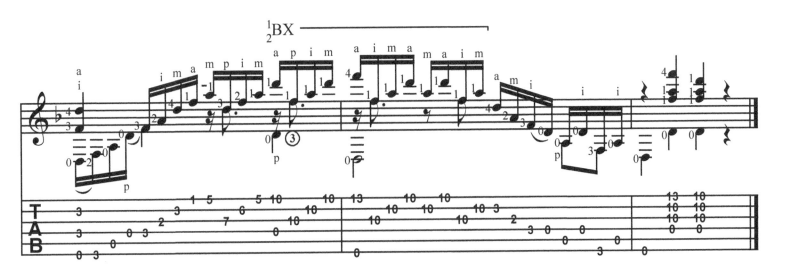

Russian Song

Peter Ilyich Tchaikovsky
(1840-1893)

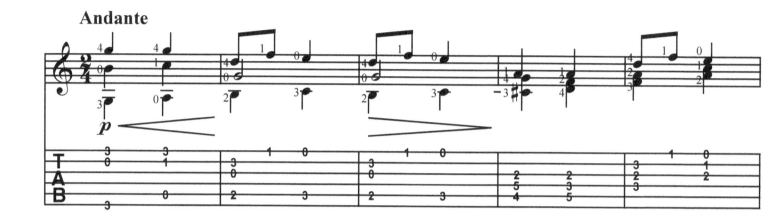

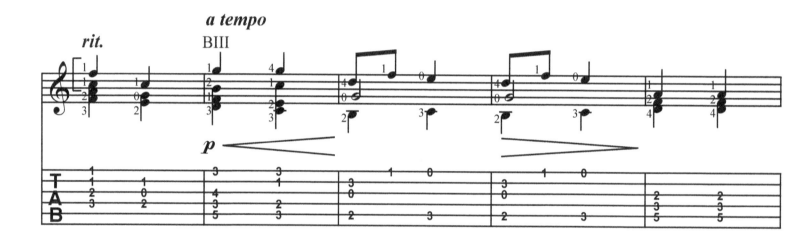

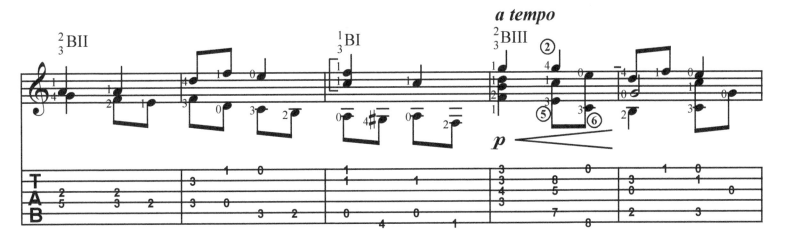

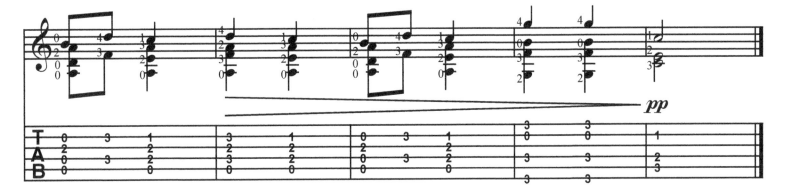

Prelude in D Major

Francisco Tárrega
(1852-1909)

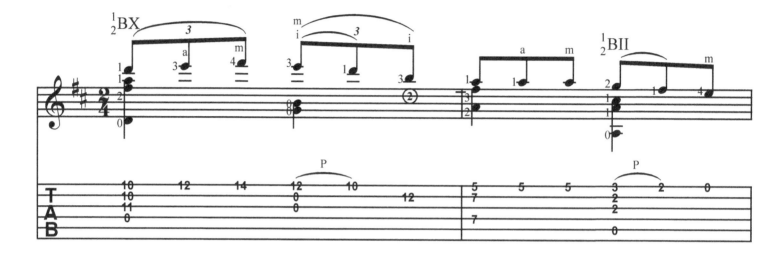

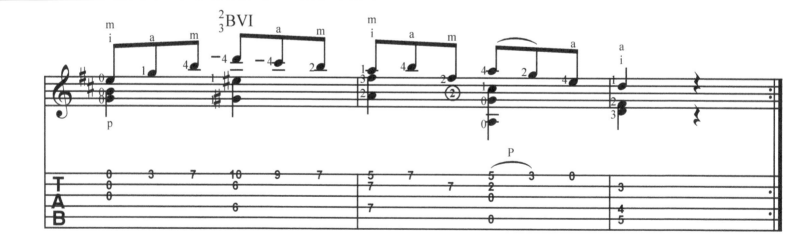

Prelude
(Endecha)

Francisco Tárrega
(1852-1909)

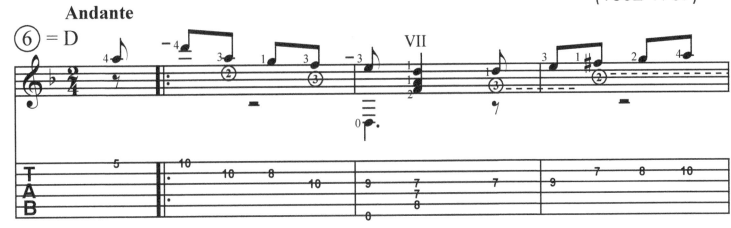

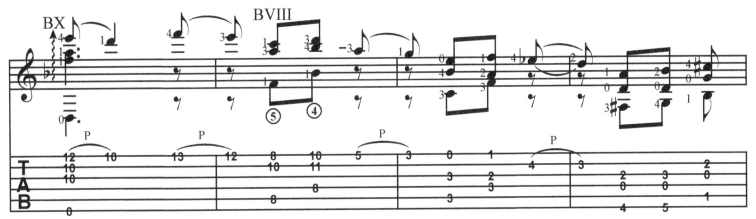

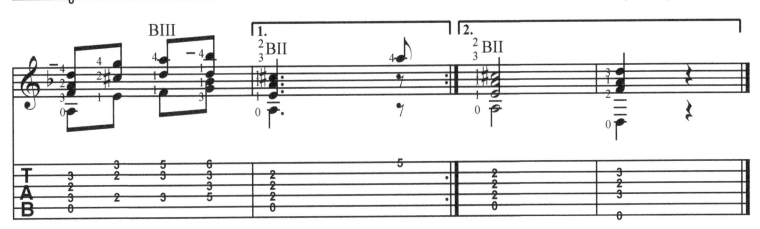

Prelude in D Minor

Francisco Tárrega
(1852-1909)

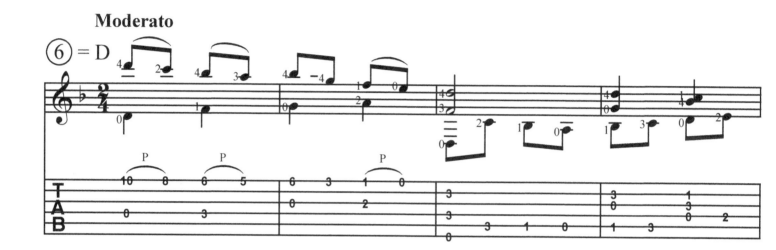

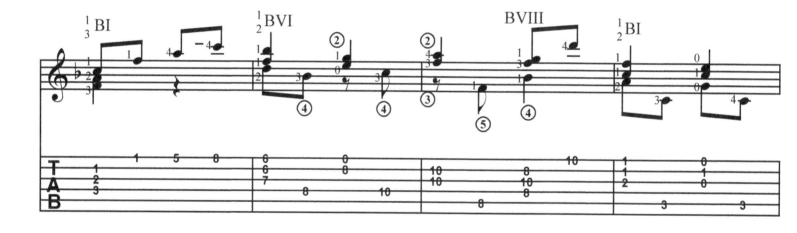

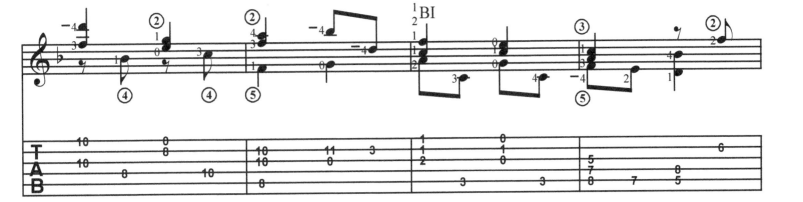

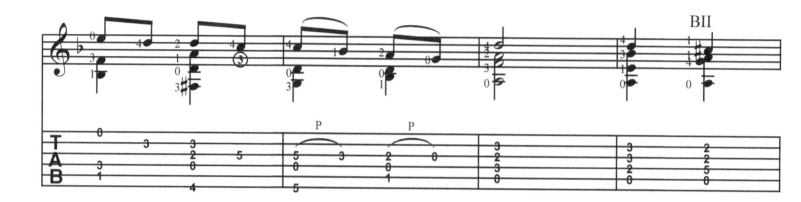

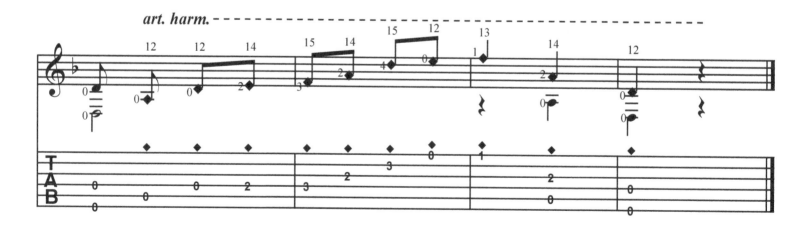

Prelude in E Major

Francisco Tárrega
(1852-1909)

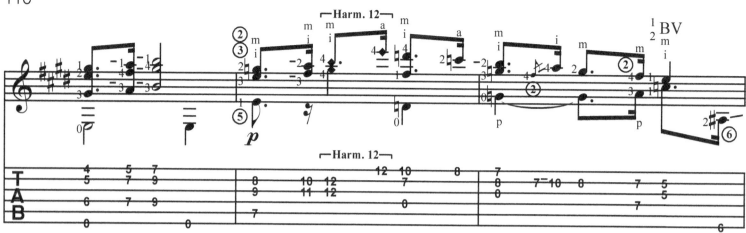

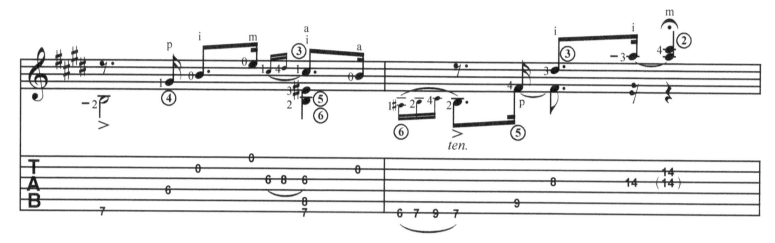

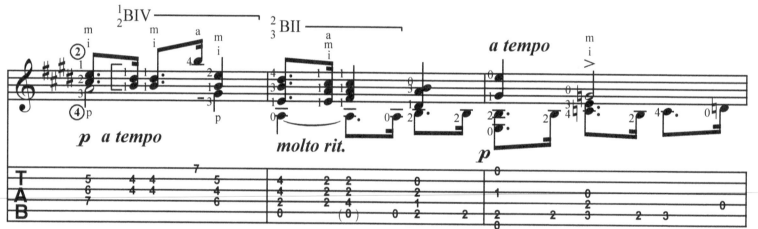

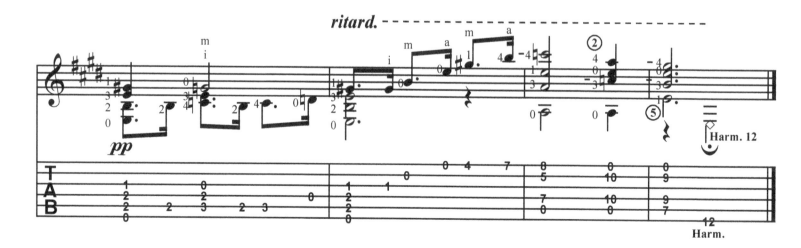

Mazurka

Francisco Tárrega
(1852-1909)

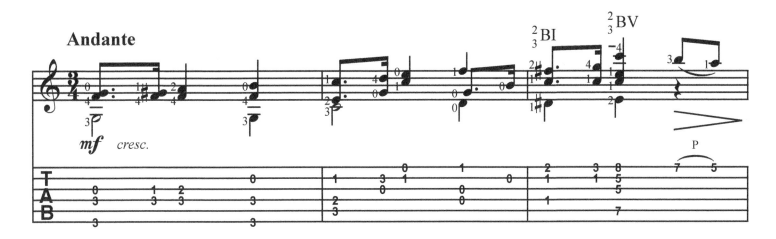

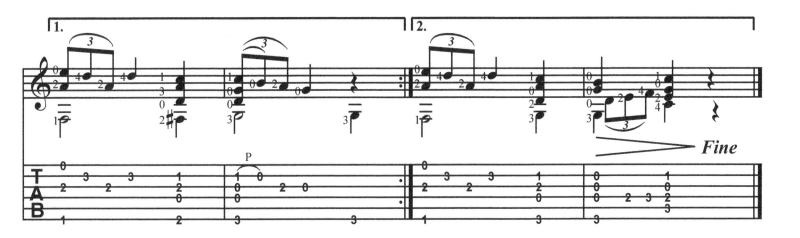

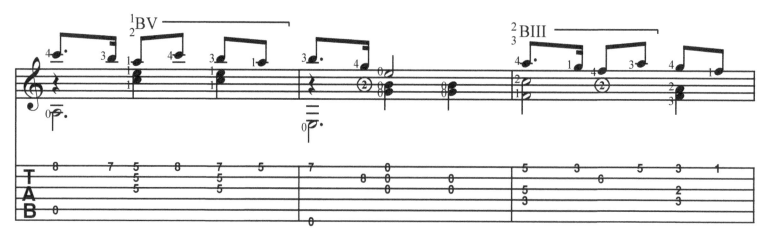

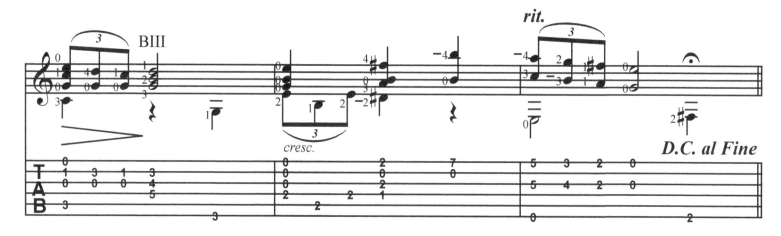